Paperback ISBN: 978-1-64873-110-5
Ebook ISBN: 978-1-64873-109-9

Printed in the United States of America

Published by:
Writer's Publishing House
Prescott, Az 86301

Cover and Interior Design by Creative Artistic Excellence Marketing
Project Management and Book Launch by Creative Artistic Excellence

Get Hired
Find a Job in 30 Days

annaelizabethjudd.com

By Lizzy McNett

Table of Contents

Introduction

The power of thought is an incredible innate genetic tool all humans possess. The key is learning to unlock its potential. As you read the pages of this book, the intent is to equip each person with the desire to dominate their dreams.

When you acquire the knowledge of how your thoughts can create wealth, it's game over. Success emanates from you, and you can turn what you love to do into money.

We are all leaders in some form or fashion. My question is, are you leading or just talking the talk? If no one is following, then check the path you are pursuing.

People want to follow leaders. In the 21st century, humans seek new methods and techniques to overcome the challenges of life. Leaders study research and learn how to maximize their unique gifts in such a way that success is the only outcome. The results allow them to live the American dream.

People often get confused about what the American dream represents. Some misconceptions are owning a fancy house and buying lots of tangible items. All of those things are fantastic goals, but the ultimate target should be waking up every morning and doing what you love. Hence, a successful entrepreneur lives life on his or her terms and dictates their worth. No one tells them when to clock in for work, what days a week they have off, and most importantly, that person's worth is not decreed by how much they make per hour for someone else's accomplishments.

The power of thought begins with your ability to tap into the genetic material you possess. Look inside yourself and ask this priceless question: What is my genetically designed purpose, the one thing I execute with ease? That I can perform with precision? Then, focus on how you can maximize this life assignment.

My instructions start by creating a powerful and dominant mental mindset that will allow you to focus and concentrate on your purpose. You should be so focused on what you were born to do that others wonder whether you are possessed or obsessed with reaching your dreams and goals. It is after you achieve this level of concentration that your innate desires surface and success becomes real.

I mentor and coach talented writers every day. My gift allows me to help these individuals birth their dreams. I strive to accomplish my visions in every area of life.

My motto is: "You get strength by helping others succeed. Books are the creators of knowledge."

Your Unemployment Story Begins
You Dictate How It Ends

The First Day of Your New Beginning

You got the call, or they just walked in and gave the announcement: you have been laid off. Whether it's a downsize, company merge, or restructure does not matter, today was your last day. As your heart stands still, the lump in your throat begins to swell, and you hold back the tears to escape the terrifying situation, visions of the future flash before your eyes. The hopeless emotions that go along with fear riddle your mind. A numb feeling takes hold while you clear out your desk and prepare to leave the office for the last time. As you struggle to keep control of your composure, someone makes mention of the situation, distracting you and causing the flood of pent-up stress to overflow in sight of everyone in the room.

You are not alone. Thousands of Americans across the country live in constant fear of losing their job every day. Companies even give the news on holidays or an employee's day off. Either way, unemployment is not a joke to anyone.

The answers you seek are in the pages of this book. Get Hired was designed to give you a step-by-step guide that mentors you through each layer involved in gaining employment in today's job market. The most critical phase is just ahead. You must rebuild your employment potential through this transition.

Unemployment is an equal opportunity experience; unemployment bypasses no one. You must not give up or quit. The key is to stay and fight; it's never too late.

Develop Your Natural Dynamic Potential

People spend hours in quiet places meditating on the meaning of life. Humans struggle on a daily basis to discover their true purpose. To create massive results and become a driving force in a prospective field, you must apply your talents, skills, and abilities.

Real success comes when people learn how to discover their Natural Dynamic Potential. Young people are not taught these skills. Therefore, most of us are at a disadvantage as life progresses. But, that does not mean you should stop trying. Today is your day! Make the most of what you have and work to reach your goals. If Michael Jordan, Tiger Woods, and Bill Gates found their power place, so can you.

From the time we are young, our lives developed from a foundation of some education, usually public schooling. Then we move on to college or a trade school to build more education, higher skills, abilities, and expertise in our career field. But it's all acquired to pour everything we have into someone else's dream. At this point, we are learning about what someone else knows, not what we know. You then let other people identify your talents in an interview, hire you, and incorporate your efforts to assist them in becoming wealthy. Don't get me wrong; it was great to grow up and allow corporate America to pay you a salary and in return let you live a certain quality of life. My question is, what quality of life are they allowing you to live?

The Industrial Age, while fantastic, it is the past. Now that we are traveling at the speed of thought, the Industrial Age and what worked fifteen years ago is becoming irrelevant. The free enterprise world has changed drastically. It allows people to turn what they love to do into money. The next generation made a conscious decision that they are not going to work for some company for twenty or thirty years like a dog, retire, get a gold watch and two years later have a heart attack and die.

Individuals are finally asking how to maximize their skills to create life leverage. The answer is simple: perfect your special gift. Then you will live the American dream, and I don't mean becoming a homeowner, either.

The modern apocalypse has changed the way humans see life on the planet. People want to get paid for doing what they love, plus make a handsome profit. By prospering from work you love, everyone wins, both buyer and seller. When you work or partner with like-minded individuals, overflowing abundance reveals itself to all parties.

The power to lead comes when you tap into the power within. This happens when you look inside yourself and ask the priceless question, "Who am I?"

My instruction creates a powerful mindset to help you concentrate on your purpose. Success becomes an obsession. Your passion gives you the freedom to break the chains of societal pressures to get a real job, and the operative word here is "job." Anyone who loves what they do for a living will never work a day in their life. Dedicate yourself to you and your company.

We are all leaders in some shape, form, or fashion. If the past is not working, we must change the future.

I want to share a foolproof formula designed to help people discover their life assignment. The method was created to impact and empower you with the tools and resource you will need to maximize your potential.

Vision - Put your dreams and goals on the plasma screen of your mind. Concentrate on whatever you want to accomplish as a leader. You must start with the end in mind. Focus on the result; the challenges are mere speed bumps that won't hinder your goals if you don't let them.

Visual connections create an energy field with your thoughts driving passion into your purpose. Have you ever met anyone who is excited about their recent experience and wants to tell the world? It is that place which will connect you to your life assignment, your PURPOSE.

The past created your current path. Companies are reaping the benefits of your production, leaving you to wonder when you will take the lead. Once you learn to enable a visionary frame of mind, you will be a frontrunner.

Purpose–The more challenging question is discovering your innate skills. Think about the one thing you would do without getting paid, something no one else can compete with you with. It's the driving force behind your expertise. You don't have to think to perform such actions. Everyone has their purpose, so what's yours? I have also learned that some people have a multitude of talents.

One must scan the recesses of their mind to seek what excites the soul. The key to the equation is that the task is effortless. Other people will be amazed by your talents and wonder how you accomplish such work with ease. Discovering the one unique skill elevates you to the power place, your connection with the Universe. Now it's time to develop the discipline, and demonstrate and dominate your life passion.

Passion–Once you learn what supercharges your drive, the hunger to achieve greatness stimulates your inner being.

The mind is the control tower for who you become. Everything you do begins with your thought process. Imagine the power you have in your mind; focus on the one thing without limitation, and you will achieve every goal set for yourself. But remember, whether it's good or bad is moot because it all starts with your initial mindset.

The process starts with positive thought conversations. You rehearse them until they take over your subconscious. Discipline is a powerful tool when used properly. The focus brings forth your purposeful power zone.

Power—The amount of drive necessary to reach your power zone depends on the time dedicated to accomplishing your dreams and goals.

An explosion takes place in every area of your life when you reach this point. Whatever area you focus on begins to overflow with abundance. Take for example Oprah Winfrey, Tiger Woods, Bill Gates, Donald Trump, or Michael Jordan. When these individuals hit their power place, an explosion occurred, launching them to the top of their fields. Each of these people affected every person around them, just by discovering their life assignment. Your passion is driven by your purpose, propelling you to your power zones.

My friend, you can live your dreams. It may not be to that extent, but take the lead, make up your mind, and say, "If not me, then who? If not now, then when, if not here, then where?" It's up to you.

The only thing that's keeping you from experiencing the power of leadership in your life is YOU. The Employee Mentality has hurt America. It's time to bring forth a new mindset called the "Entrepreneur Mentality." Stop thinking like an employee.

What is the Employee Mentality? It's simple: when someone goes to work and only does what's necessary. These are the people who appear to look busy. They accomplish nothing and leave someone else to pick up the slack. As an example, Jane Doe, "I don't care if anyone else walks through that door or buys anything. I'd be happy if no one else comes in the rest of the day."

The unproductive hours cost the company money. A lack of manufacturing leads to downsizes and merges. This in return brings about layoffs and crossfires due to the lack of revenue.

The Entrepreneur Mindset is the sought-after mentality when approaching the employment process and other facets of life. This concept revolutionizes the way we obtain employment. It is the frame of mind to understand we are all in business for ourselves even if we are working with (did you notice that I did not say "working for") someone else.

Unlock the Executive Suite of Your Life

> ➤ "(Your Name) Incorporated,"

What company is still there after they lay you off?

> ➤ "(Your Name) Incorporated,"

What company is still there after they decide your department is no longer necessary?

> ➤ "(Your Name) Incorporated,"

What company is with you in the midst of those major stressful moments? You know, those moments when life wakes you up at three o'clock in the morning?

The moments you ease out of bed, go into the living room and stare at curtains with tears rolling down your face, not knowing which direction right, or left?

What company can you count on?

"(Your Name) Incorporated."

It is during these times you learn who you are, along with the people in your life. No matter what the situation, we are the only stable foundation to stand on. Your company can attract the right opportunities to overcome these employment challenges. Am I the only one who has ever been in this state of mind? If you focus on maximizing all areas of your company and getting connected with like-minded individuals, you will be successful.

Why are companies no longer looking for individuals with the Employee Mentality? It is simply outdated. They are searching for those with the Entrepreneur Mentality, because these employees will positively affect their bottom line. Those who choose to work for someone else are material assets.

The Entrepreneur Mentality Statement

"If I'm going to work to give 110% to my company, '(Your Name) Incorporated' every day, the company I'm connected with (my job) can't help but make money."

When you invest in a career, the result is leverage to reach your business destiny. An expanding mindset exists in Americans that being laid off is a personal decision, but in fact, it's only business. The company is in business to make money, period. If demand for their product drops, employee cuts are the next step. Instead of panicking, use the time wisely to choose an alternate path. I am going to provide you with the direction and tools needed to get your career situation on track.

Food for Thought:

Have you ever quit a job? I have. Think about it; it was a business decision. The only difference here is, the shoe is on the other foot. Regain your footing and follow me.

Ensure that your resume is complete and up-to-date. Prepare for different interview questions and research the company. If you have no experience, consider doing internships or volunteer work. Apply for jobs that fit your skills and interests. In interviews, sell your qualifications and stress that you look forward to getting trained, learning, and growing.

The key to employment success is an up-to-date resume. Your resume is an essential distillation of who you are, where you come from, and what you can offer. Here are a few tips to consider:

➤ Never make up information on a resume; it can come back to haunt you later.

➤ Look at a variety of recent, relevant job descriptions. Use similar language to describe your skills and accomplishments on your resume.

➤ Use active verbs when describing what you did at your last job. Make the sentence as tight and active as possible.

➤ Proofread. Review your resume several times for grammatical or spelling errors. Even something as simple as a typo could negatively impact your ability to land an interview, so pay close attention to what you've left on the page. Get someone to review the resume.

➤ Keep the formatting classic and to the point. How your resume looks is almost as important as how it reads. Use a simple font (such as Times New Roman, Arial or Bevan), black ink on white or ivory colored paper, and wide margins (about 1" on each side). Avoid bold or italic lettering. Ensure your name and contact information are clearly and prominently displayed.

You have just been promoted to President and CEO of your own company. The name of that company/corporation is "Me Incorporated."

Whatever your name is "(Your Name) Incorporated."

Your company is affected by everything it's connected to, which influences every person including yourself, along with your thought's ideas and actions. The most important company in the world is your empire.

Many structured interviews, particularly those at large companies, start with a question like "Tell me about yourself." The interviewer doesn't want to hear about grade school or growing up. The answer should be, the work-related experience since you were an adult. Keep it within two minutes. The interviewer wants to understand your background, your accomplishments, why you want to work at this company and what your future goals are.

Keep your answers brief — between 30 seconds and two minutes — and have the basics memorized so you don't stammer when you're asked to describe yourself. You don't want to sound like a robot, either, so get the structure down. Learn to improvise. Practice your elevator pitch out loud to someone who can give you feedback.

An elevator pitch is useful when you're networking. Use it at a party, or anywhere with a group of strangers. It gives them an overview of your message. In a networking situation, as opposed to a job interview, keep the elevator pitch to 30 seconds or less.

Make a list of work-related skills you'd like to learn. Your employer will be interested in hearing about how you intend to become a better employee. Choose which skills you are comfortable with in the position. Find some books and upcoming conferences that would significantly improve your abilities. In an interview, tell the employer what you're reading and learning and that you'd like to continue doing so. Here is a list of critical job skills that are wanted by employers. Job-seekers must learn them to land a good job, and more importantly, keep it.

- ➤ **Logical thinking and information handling:** Most businesses regard the ability to handle and organize information to produce practical solutions as a top skill. They value the ability to make sensible solutions regarding a spending proposal or an internal activity.
- ➤ **Technological ability:** Most job openings will require people who are computer literate or know how to operate different machines and office equipment. Whether it's a PC or multi-function copier and scanner does not matter. It doesn't mean employers demand people who are technology graduates — knowing the basic principles of using current technology is sufficient.
- ➤ **Efficient communicating:** Employers tend to value and hire people who can express their thoughts efficiently through verbal and written communication. People who easily land a good job are usually those who are adept at speaking and writing.
- ➤ **Strong interpersonal skills:** The work environment consists of many personalities with different backgrounds and skill levels.

Therefore it is essential to possess effective communication abilities, no matter the setting.

You might be asked to describe problems you've encountered in the past and how you handled them, or you'll be given a hypothetical situation and asked what you would do. You might also be asked questions looking for negative information. They want to know how you'll perform when faced with obstacles in the interviewing process. Be able to give honest, detailed examples from your past, even if the question is hypothetical (e.g., "I would contact the customer directly, based on my experience in a different situation in which the customer was very pleased to receive a phone call from the supervisor"). You might find yourself listing facts — if so, remember that in this kind of interview, you need to tell a story. Some questions you might be asked are:

- ➢ "Describe a time you had to work with someone you didn't like."
- ➢ "Tell me about a time when you had to stick by a decision, even though it made you unpopular."

- "Give us an example of something particularly innovative you did that made a difference in the workplace."
- "How would you handle an employee who's consistently late?"

Don't just do an Internet search, memorize their mission, and be done with it. Remember that you're competing with lots of other candidates for a few or a single position. You may not be able to change your natural intelligence or the skills that you bring to the table, but you can always change your work ethic. Work harder than everyone else by researching the company or companies you wish to work for as if your life depended on it.

If it's a retail company, visit a few of their stores, observe the customers, and even strike up a few conversations. Talk to existing employees — ask them what it's like working there, how long has the position been open, and what you can do to increase your chances of getting the position. Become familiar with the history of the company. Who started it? Where? Who runs it now? Be creative!

An informational interview is when you invite a contact or a professional out to lunch or coffee and ask them questions without the expectation of getting a job. These meetings are great for networking, expanding contacts lists, and gaining tips and tricks from professionals who are on the ground.

Have lots of questions prepared:

- ➤ "What's a normal day like for you?"
- ➤ "What are the advantages of your job?"
- ➤ "What might you have done differently?"

When the interview is done, ask them politely for additional contacts. If you impress them enough, they could even hire you or refer you to someone who could hire you.

The best companies to work for tend to rely heavily on employee referrals. Make a list of all of your friends, relatives, and acquaintances. Contact them one by one and ask them if they know of any openings for which they could recommend you. Don't be too humble or apologetic. Tell them what you're looking for, but let them know you're flexible and open to suggestions. Don't be picky about jobs at this stage, a connection can get your foot in the door, and you can negotiate pay or switch positions once you've gained experience and established your reputation.

Touch base with all of your references. The purpose of this is twofold. You can ask them for leads, and you'll be refreshing their memory of you. (Hopefully their memories of you are good ones, or else you shouldn't be listing them as references.) If a potential employer calls them, they won't hesitate as much when remembering you. Offer all of your references a copy of your latest resume.

Keep in mind that, as with dating, "weak" personal connections are often the best way to find a new job. They expand your network beyond options you're already aware of. You probably know all about your sister's company, and you know that if they were hiring, she would tell you; but what about your sister's friend's company? Don't be afraid to ask the friend of a friend or another slightly removed acquaintance for recommendations during your job search.

If you aren't already, start volunteering for an organization that focuses on things that pertain to your passions. You may start out doing tedious or easy work, but as you stick around and demonstrate your commitment, you'll be given more responsibilities. Not only will you be helping others, but you'll also be gaining references. Emphasize your volunteer experience on your resume. Companies that treat their employees well tend to favor candidates who help the community in some way.

Internships may fall into this category, or they may be paid. An internship can get your foot in the door. Many companies prefer to hire within the company. Even if you're far removed from your twenties or your college days, the willingness to work for little or no money shows companies that you're serious about putting in the work, learning the skills, and getting ahead.

Believe it or not, volunteer positions and internships can lead to jobs. In today's economy, many companies are turning to internships as a cost-effective way to vet potential future employees. Many companies simply don't have the money or resources to take a stab in the dark and offer a job to someone who isn't tested. If you put in hard work, demonstrate your ability to solve problems, and keep your chin up, your value to the company might be too big for them to pass up.

Locate a specific person who can help you (usually the human resources or hiring manager at a company or organization you're interested in). Call that person and ask if they are hiring, but do not become discouraged from getting a no. Ask what kind of qualifications they look for or if they have an apprentice or government-sponsored work program. Ask if you can send your resume indicating what field you want. Tell them whether you would accept a lesser job and work your way up.

Reflect on the phone call; what went well, and what needs work. Consider writing out some standard answers on your list of skills so you can speak fluently. You may need to get some additional training to break into your chosen field. None of this means you cannot get a good job, only that you need to become better prepared to do so.

Visit the company or business in person. There's a saying among employers: "People don't hire resumes; people hire people."

Don't underestimate the value of personal relationships. Go to the company or business where you think you might want to work, bring your resume, and ask to speak to the Human Resources manager about job opportunities. If you make an excellent personal impression on the HR manager, you've done your job. She/he will have connected your face to a resume and will have a much better idea of your natural intelligence, persistence, and likability. People don't always hire the person best suited for the job; people often hire the person they like the best.

There's a difference between making phone calls and going to interviews thinking "I'm looking for a job" versus "I'm here to do the work you need to have done." When you're looking to get a job, you're expecting someone to give something to you, so you focus on impressing them. Yes, it's imperative to make a good impression, but it's even more important to demonstrate your desire and ability to help. Everything you write should be preceded silently by the statement "This is how I can help your business succeed."

If you've moved around a lot, be prepared to offer a good reason for it. Otherwise, you'll need to make a good case why you are not moving any longer. A company doesn't want to hire someone with wanderlust who still wants to relocate.

Be prepared to outline why you are where you are today, how long you intend to stay, and why. Give specific reasons like, "This country has the best school systems in the continent. I have a daughter who might find the cure for cancer," or "I was drawn to this area because of its cutting edge innovation for business. I want to be a part of that." The more details, names, and specifics, the better.

Find jobs that fit your skill-set and interests, rather than focusing on the wrong kind of work. Learn the skills to improve your job abilities, and build your skills before seeking employment in an unknown field. Many companies promote from within, which gives you the opportunity to work up the ladder.

Make a list of all of your skills, determine which kinds of businesses and industries need them most (ask around for advice if necessary) and find companies that will benefit from having you and your skills around. Sometimes, you can get enjoyment out of a career that wasn't on your radar. Always keep an open mind.

Explore the nature of jobs to fit your personality and salary requirements. Otherwise, you'll have spent a significant amount of time finding a day job — but you dread getting up every morning. You must be realistic with your expectations, but always be open to new opportunities.

Sell the qualifications you have, and say you look forward to honing your skills, getting trained, and growing into the rest. Don't panic, and don't count yourself out if you don't have 100% of the things in a job description. The company will advertise job listings that explain their ideal candidate. Just appear well mannered, sit upright yet relaxed, don't frown or grimace, and be positive. They want to see someone who is proactive and leaning slightly forward, showing interest. Make the right impression based on optimism and confidence. Don't settle back in your chair or get too comfortable. Be alert while not acting too nervous or desperate.

A resume is a self-advertisement. When done correctly, it shows how your skills, experience, and achievements match the requirements of the job you want. This Get Hired guide provides three free samples on which you can base your resume. It will also walk you through setting up and laying out the content to highlight your skills and grab the reader's attention.

Format your text. The text is the first thing a potential employer will notice. For that reason, it is essential to make the right first impression. Choose a professional font in size 11 or 12. Times New Roman is the classic serif font, while Arial and Calibri are two of the better choices for sans-serif. Yahoo cites Helvetica as the best font even though sans serif fonts are more common. Many individuals find Times New Roman harder to read on a screen. If you are emailing your resume, consider using Georgia instead for a more readable serif font.

You can use multiple fonts for different parts of your resume, but limit it to two. Instead of changing between fonts, try bolding or italicizing specific selections of text instead.

The font size for your header and the introduction to a section can be 14 or 16, but otherwise, you should choose 11 or 12.

Your text should always be printed in solid black ink. Make sure to deactivate any hyper-links (like to your email, address, and phone number) so that they don't print in blue or another color that isn't black.

Set up the page. Your page should have one-inch margins all the way around with 1.5 or 2-point line spacing. The body of your resume will be aligned to the left, and your header should be centered at the top of your page. (Never use justification; it causes wide spaces between the words.)

Create your heading, the section at the top of your resume which gives your contact information including your name, address, email, and phone number. Your name should be slightly larger - either 14 or 16-point font. List your home and cell phone numbers.

Decide on a layout. There are three general formats for creating a resume: chronological, functional, or combination. Your work history and the type of job you are applying for will determine the layout style.

Chronological resumes are for showing steady growth in a particular career field. These are best for someone applying for a job within their career-path to show an increase of responsibility over time.

Functional resumes are focused on skills and experience rather than job history. These are used for someone who may have holes in their work history or who have gained experience from being self-employed for a time.

Combination resumes are, as it sounds, a combination of both a chronological and a functional resume. These are used to show off specific skills and how they were acquired. If you have developed a particular skill set from working in a variety of related fields, then this is the best resume option for you.

Writing a Chronological Resume

List your employment history. As this is a chronological resume, your jobs should be listed in reverse chronological order with your most recent employment first. Include the name of the company, its location, your title, your duties, and responsibilities while working there, and the dates that you were employed.

It may be beneficial to list your title first to show off your position in each job. You can also choose to list the company name first. Regardless of what you choose, be consistent down your entire list.

For each listing, write a "Major Achievements" or "Accomplishments" section with a brief description.

Provide your education history. Same as with your jobs, you should list all of your education in reverse chronological order with your most recent schooling first. Include any college degrees, trade schools, or apprenticeships you might have participated in. If you graduated with a degree, list the name of the degree as well as the year you received it. If you have not graduated, state the years you attended the program as well as an expected graduation date. For each listing, give the university/program name, their address, and your degree or area of study.

If you had a cumulative GPA of 3.5 or higher, be sure to list it along with your school/degree information.

Give unique qualifications or skills. Once you've listed the most important information - your work experience and education - you can add anything else you find valuable. Create a section titled "Special Skills" or "Unique Qualifications" that lists these things.

If you are fluent in more than one language, list the multiple languages here. Be sure to make a note of your knowledge level - for example, beginner, intermediate, novice, advanced, fluent, etc.

Day One

Reflect, Regroup, Refocus, Recharge

Reflect on your success. Stay positive and productive, and revisit the accomplishments with your previous employer. No matter how small the check or how negative the experience, I want you to be grateful for the opportunity.

Be thankful, and write a gratitude list for the opportunity. Everything you experienced is a part of your destined assignment in this universe. The positive energy should bring fortune to your future endeavors. Reflect, but don't stay long. Get up and regroup. The experience should bring happiness if you keep an open mind.

Many times, we have hoped and prayed for something to come along that would allow us the freedom to get paid good money doing what we love to do, every single day. I'm talking about those things that burn inside, and every time you get a chance to do them, your entire being is supercharged with what I call a shot of motivational Blue Kryptonite.

The next step dictates a plan to refocus on things that matter. In other words, where do you go from here? What is the next level? What changes can be made to avoid this situation in the future?

The answers lie in the pages ahead. It's not too late; the time is now. Get on a mission to create an understanding of the success you want to achieve. Create a daily goal and stay driven. Plan to make it happen no matter what.

Example: You know paying your mortgage or rent is the only way to keep a roof over your family's head, and you just lost your job. You will do everything in your power to maintain a stable household environment. Use this as a motivation supercharge for your spirit and career search.

"If you want something you've never had, do something you've never done." – James Amps III

Desperate moments can make us impulsive, but this is not a time to be rash. Slow down, breathe and choose wisely. Who do you have in place that can help you meet your emergency needs if necessary? Leave the pity party behind, lace up your bootstraps and go to work. Are you going to create additional streams of income to offset your expenses and keep this from happening? Are you going to create a massive home-based business that will give you the opportunity to get out of the rat race where the average lifespan of a job is between 3.5 and 7 years?

No matter how many times they are laid off, the Employee Mentality rears its ugly head again. Once you face facts and reflect, please regroup and refocus on what it is that you want. It's time to recharge.

A complete overhaul to vitalize your passion will call forth your hidden strengths: "It's my turn! I've had all I can stand, and I can't stand anymore!"

Once you get to this point, you will be super recharged for action. Now you are prepared to take total control of your destiny, by any means necessary. Who can help you get there? Let's go! I'm ready to lead you on the path to employee empowerment.

Day Two

You Are the Boss

Get up and dressed for work as usual. In fact, you are working, just for a different boss. If you are seeking employment, that is your job. Be someone who is driven. You are your new boss and success is always possible when you believe.

Remember, the President and CEO of your company is in total control of every department within your internal and external corporate empire. Take a moment to think and meditate on your newly found position within a multi-million-dollar operation. Why do I quote excessive monetary amounts like this when you have not come anywhere near that kind of money? You were paid an hourly wage to support someone else's dream. You helped them become wealthy, whether you know it or not. You used your time and talents to assist many people in enjoying a lifestyle that far exceeds your own. So, if you helped them in doing this, don't you think that it's time to give yourself credit for some of that hard work?

Incorporate the Entrepreneur Mentality as you get ready to go on tomorrow's assignment.

Let's Get Started

Personal Assessment of YOU.

- ➤ Name:
- ➤ Address:
- ➤ City: State: Zip:
- ➤ Phone:
- ➤ e-mail:
- ➤ Position (s) sought:
- ➤ Are you currently unemployed?
- ➤ If yes, for how long?
- ➤ Please complete the questionnaire below
  Yes   No
- ➤ Have you checked the Help Wanted Ads?
- ➤ Positions in your field of experience?
- ➤ Positions in different fields?
- ➤ Do you subscribe to or purchase the local (esp. Sunday) papers?
- ➤ Did you create a new resume since beginning your most recent job?
- ➤ Internet Searches?
- ➤ Have you created more than one resume?

Please include the features of your resume:

- ➢ Objectives
- ➢ Education
- ➢ Experience
- ➢ Referrals?
- ➢ Do you always include a cover letter?
- ➢ Do you always respond to ads by their stated deadline?
- ➢ Does your résumé/cover letter highlight your qualifications?
- ➢ Have you ever gone door-to-door inquiring about jobs?
- ➢ Have you ever used mass mailings to look for a job?
- ➢ Do you keep accurate records of all your job-search efforts?
- ➢ What methods does your job-search include?
- ➢ List all ads you have responded to (who, what, where, when).
- ➢ Did you send follow up letters, cards, and résumés?
- ➢ List your in-depth research on targeted firms
- ➢ Did you directly contact firms that do not have openings?

- Have you ever researched government listings for jobs?
- Have you ever worked with headhunters/employment agencies?
- Have you ever used the services provided by Unemployment?
- Have you ever used Internet/Web-based job boards?

  Yes or No
- Are you/have you been networking?

With whom?

- Family
- Friends
- Co-workers
- Alumni
- Colleagues
- Peers
- Clubs
- Church
- Other

- Have you done any interning or volunteering to research jobs?
- Have you done any targeted mailings?
- Have you done any targeted telephoning?

➤ Do you use any personal marketing materials other than your résumé?

➤ Describe them:

➤ Are you positioned to take advantage of emerging opportunities?

➤ Do you do anything to discover unpublished job openings?

➤ If yes, what?

Do you know your personal, intrinsic strengths? List your strengths:

     1.

     2.

     3.

     4.

➤ Have you considered going back to school to enter a new field?

➤ Have you practiced your interviewing skills?

➤ Do you know how to ask for the job during an interview?

➤ Are you willing to use a new method and new tools?

There is no one particular reason people get the wrong results when it comes to job hunting. You can do everything correctly and not get the job. The reason could be a poor career match, lack of experience, education, or your skills don't fit HR's perceived necessities. Other times, it is those things that we cannot speak about: age, sex, religion, etc. In any case, months out of work or years spent underemployed are truly painful and discouraging. If only there was a better way! **There is!**

The 30-Day Job Search Change Method builds on the work you've already done (creating your résumé and cover letters, sending them out to everyone you know, responding to ads, and so on). It is a supplement, not a replacement, for your primary work on job/career change. But it is an alteration that works. Like a fuel additive that improves mileage or a vitamin that gives you extra energy and stamina.

The 30-Day Job Search Change Method can make all the difference. You can get interviews, along with the positions you seek. It builds upon your strengths and your monetary contributions.

Assignment #1

Make a contact list

Start with a list of everyone you know that can help you in reaching your employment goals. Include people you have worked with, family members, and friends and meditate on which people have connections with others that can assist you. Write the names down and go about obtaining pertinent contact information. Building a massive network of people that you can work with is a great way to pool resources and expand your inner circle.

My List:

It's not what you know, it's who you know. Our minds are like sponges, and if driven, we can learn anything. The right open door is what you seek.

These are the people that you approach and say: "Hi Bridgett, I'm looking for a career opportunity in your field. Can you be of any assistance?"

Inform them of the position you want, ask how things are going and see if you can reciprocate the connection.

These people graduated to your official, "I'm going to help you become a member of the career and business success club."

Time to Take Note:

Day Three

Form Powerful Habits

Assignment #2

Make a list of goals, career fields, and options and complete a master application.

Goals

Dream Big! Start with what you ultimately want out of life and the whole employment experience. Then work backward to your current situation. What do you need to do today, next week, next month, and next year to get to where you want to be? The answers to those questions make up your goals.

Career Field

Make a list of career fields and decide which ones interest you the most and incorporate your skill set, knowledge, and experience. Tap the areas that excite you and quicken your spirit, then place them into categories as they relate to your career goals.

Career Options

Use a search engine and type in the career field of interest to pull up a list of viable jobs that are hiring in your area.

Mind you: We are only researching at this point. Also, never underestimate the power of freedom; your willingness to relocate could be your ticket to a bright future.

Reference Websites

Complete your profile and attach your resume to ALL of these that apply:

- ➤ Getmymomajob.com
- ➤ Getmydadajob.com
- ➤ Getmyvetajob.com
- ➤ Careerbuilder.com
- ➤ Indeed.com
- ➤ jobing.com

These are my favorite, but you can pick your own. Plus, there are thousands of remote jobs, if you are seeking that type of option. Legitimate jobs with W-2 income; companies like Amazon, Intuit, utility companies, Sears, Aon, Hertz Penske, and many others.

Complete a Master Application

The concept of having one source for all your information eliminates having to scramble for previous employment records each time you go on a job interview. It can also be used as a reference when filling out online applications. Let's work smarter to gain employment.

Computer Assignment

Do an email listing of all the people that you know with the power of influence and their contact information. It gives you the opportunity to connect with these people and have them distribute your resume, aka networking.

Day 4

Format Your Resume

Chronological Resume

Use this outline as your master resume with work history in a one or two-page format. *Google search*: Sample Chronological Resume

Sections of a Resume

- ➤ Heading
- ➤ Name, address, one phone number, email address

Make sure that the email address makes a good impression by representing your professionalism. Personal email addresses for buddy lists are not recommended. Get a new email address for just your employment information. Using your name is an affirmative action toward remembering you.

The position must be listed in the objective. When an employer is reviewing resumes, they are sorting for no longer than eight to ten seconds before deciding whether to continue the review or to dispose of them.

My Objective:

Summary

The concise synopsis of who you are must contain three essential elements.

> ➤ Years of experience

Ex: Six years of experience in the related field of retail customer service.

> ➤ Skills and expertise

Ex: Proficient in MS Word, Excel, PowerPoint, Outlook and Adobe Acrobat.

> ➤ Communication skills

Always write with clarity and use proper English. Before this section is complete, make sure the resume is reviewed for punctuation, capitalization, and grammatical errors. You don't want to present yourself as an articulate person and have these errors exist. It will land your resume in the trash.

Education / Certification

If the job description lists an educational accomplishment, display it in the summary. Meaning, if it requires a degree then list what type of degree you obtained. List only the degree relevant to the position. Put any other information in the education section towards the bottom of your resume.

If the field requires a certification, list the certification that is required to get the job. No other certifications are needed if they are not relevant to the position that you are applying for.

About You

List your characteristics that make you ideal for the position. Eighty percent of employers hire from within, and most of them give a lot of weight to the traits that fit the job.

Ex: Detail oriented, able to work in a multi-tasking environment, able to work under pressure, enjoys working with people and meeting their needs.

Work History

List your employment beginning with your most recent job, and give the last three jobs or employers. If this doesn't apply, then list a total of five to ten years of employment.

Write the companies' name, city, state, and several bullet points on your job duties.

Use a search engine to pull up good descriptions of your previous job titles. (Search Engine) Google Search - online for job descriptions.

Education

In this section is where you list your educational background. You need to list only one major university that you have attended. If you did not graduate, only list the school you went to and not a graduation date.

If you received a GED, do not list that. Only put the high school that you attended with city and state and the year you graduated. Things not included on a one-page resume are GPA (unless outstanding), hours of credits, and more than one university if not needed.

References Per Request

References are not necessary. If an employer wants to speak with people you know, they will say so. Type a list of your references on a separate page and use this as a template for filling out applications. You need credible business references that will positively respond to questions about you and your work ethic, job performance, timeliness, reliability, etc.

Day 5

Finish Your Chronological Resume

Stand out from the sea of applicants, choose your resume paper wisely. Spend a few dollars more and buy high-grade off-white or subtly colored paper. Print ten to twenty copies at a time and keep them in a folder or leather binder. Bring the binder, pen and scratch paper to all interviews.

Day 6

Personal Career Coaching

Find someone you can trust to review all your information and make sure everything is lined up. They must be confident and motivating.

Day 7

Format Your Functional Resume

Honestly, a cover letter is optional. Yes, it looks more professional, but if you can build a powerful brand for yourself, you won't need one. Now, you need a functional resume. It differs from the chronological resume in that it is more specific.

A functional resume is geared toward a specific field with a one-page format. Google Search: Sample Functional Resume

> ➢ Heading, Objective, Summary and Communication Skills

These sections are the same as the chronological resume example.

If the field requires a certification, list the certification that is required. No other certifications are needed if they are not relevant to the position that you are applying for.

About You

This section is the same as the chronological resume example.

Professional Related Experience

This is the area where you can give the related professional experience you have in a specific area without having to repeat what you have done for the various employers.

Professional Related History

List the companies you have worked for that will assist in validating your skills and expertise.

Ex: Employers don't know you, but they will know Exxon. List the company name, your position, and the city and state where you worked; no dates are needed.

Week Two: Day Eight

Start an Email Blast

Create a personal greeting for everyone on your list. Attend a career coaching online seminar with topics such as:

> ➢ How to create a compelling personal brand.
> ➢ How to turn what you love to do into money.
> ➢ How to turn your degree into money.
> ➢ How to leverage your skills and start your own business.

Stress Management

It is imperative you stay alert and driven to succeed in your employment search. So, get plenty of sleep, eat right and exercise.

Reference Websites: Complete the profile and attach your resume to ALL of these that apply.

> ➢ Moster.com
> ➢ Indeed.com
> ➢ Clearlyrated.com
> ➢ Careerbuilder.com

➤ Jobing.com

Day Nine

Network / Interview

Learn the art of networking and gain the confidence that will dominate a room. It's crucial at this point that you regain your atmosphere in any business setting. You are at a point right now where your arsenal is beginning to fill with job seeking weapons.

Attire

A power suit is a must for the 21st century. It's essential that you walk in bringing forth the added value and return on investment you so rightly deserve. You are getting ready to partner up in your next business venture, meaning you are strategically aligning yourself with the right company.

I cannot stress this enough!
Dress for success!

Every person should have a power suit as a part of their wardrobe, no matter what. You must look the part to get the job. You cannot go wrong with the traditional suit because you will be called upon on many occasions to represent your company. With the conventional power suit, you will be welcome in any boardroom, conference or business setting. The colors of choice are dark blue or black, and if pinstripes, make certain the stripes are light in color.

Dress Code

Business professional is a win/win clothing decision. If you are interviewing for a position in the industrial field, it's essential you understand that the dress in this area is meaningful as well.

Men: A nice pair of Dockers is excellent with a button-down shirt and sports jacket. A jacket is not necessary; slacks and a button down will work. It will say a lot about you and the respect you have for their company.

Women: Fitted black pants or a knee length black skirt with a button down or a conservative, fitted sweater is appropriate. Please remember that too much information about your social beliefs displayed by your attire is not wanted at this stage in the game. Keep it simple. Wear black polished shoes.

Men: Wear black socks and shoes with a belt to match. These items are an investment in your business wardrobe.

Women: Closed toe, black heels are seasonal and regionally decided on pantyhose. In southern, warmer states it is more acceptable to go for this archaic item. Hair must be professionally groomed.

Men: Get a fade, trim up, line up, whatever you would like to call it, and shave.

Women: Keep it simple and neat. You may pull it back or wear it down, just don't look like you are going to the club or getting out of bed.

Everyone: Go light on the jewelry and light on the accessories. Less is more when you want someone to pay attention to your skills and qualifications.

Everyone: Your perfume or cologne should be clean and simple. Do you know that an overpowering fragrance can distract, annoy, and even make a future employer nauseous? Some people have serious allergies and this must be respected in a place of business.

Stay as plain as possible with the style and lining of the suit. While a pinstripe suit can be tricky, when fitted and worn correctly it can exude confidence. You may want to refer to "Tim Gunn's Guide to Style." One ring on each hand, tongue piercing removed, multiple earrings should not be worn and any facial piercings removed. Your fingernails should presentable (a French manicure is the best).

Career Gear is a non-profit organization that assists men with a business suit for their interviews when they don't have interview attire. You can also try Dress for Success, another non-profit organization that helps women with clothing for interviews.

Examples of the Chronological Resume

Reference Per Request

Do not list your references at the bottom. Finish your resume. Remember to choose your paper wisely, make plenty of copies, put them in a folder and be organized.

Day 10

Interview Format

The next section is crucial: do not be late for an interview. Always arrive thirty minutes early, and find out your interviewer's name beforehand. If you are having difficulty pronouncing the individual's name, call the place of business several times, and ask for the person so you can get it right. **Do your homework!**

Research the companies you are interviewing with: how large they are, whether they are publicly or privately held, how they got started, and how many offices in how many countries, and incorporate these facts when appropriate during the interview.

If you accept an interview at eight o'clock, make sure you are up early and have plenty of time if you are delayed in traffic. Again, make sure you have the name of the person interviewing you and be prepared for a panel interview if the position is in the business arena. This is done to save time and speed up the selection process for the prospective company.

If they seat you in the lobby for forty-five minutes, use the time to go over your One Minute Commercial and brush up on the facts about the company you have printed in your portfolio. Be friendly to the receptionist; they could be your future co-worker. Be patient; use this time to get ready to knock the employers off their feet!

Take as little as possible with you: one portfolio with six resumes inside, the information on the company, your One Minute Commercial, and a good pen should do it. Bring a reference sheet with three business and three personal references and present it only if requested to do so.

One Minute Commercial

The interviewer will probably start by saying, "Tell me about yourself."

You will be prepared with your One Minute Commercial that you wrote and memorized. Refer to the information in your resume summary. Answer the questions below and fill in the blanks in the sample portion.

> ➢ Name and where you are from
> ➢ Career field you're applying for
> ➢ How many years of experience in that field?
> ➢ Skills and expertise in that field
> ➢ What level of written and verbal communication skills do you have?
> ➢ Education and certifications
> ➢ What kind of person you are and how it relates to the type of individual they are looking to hire?

Ex: Detail oriented, problem solver, enjoys a challenge.

Sample One Minute Commercial

My name is _____ I'm originally from _____(city),

_____ (state). I have been residing in _____for the past years, or I'm a native _____.

My career field is _____ (the job that you are applying for, or the career field you prefer).

I have _____ years of experience in the related field of _____ (the career field or job that you are applying for at this particular time).

I have an extensive background (if more than eight to ten years' experience) in the related field _____.

Skills & Expertise

I'm proficient or advanced in MS Word, Excel, Access, Outlook, PowerPoint, and I type 40 wpm. (If your typing speed is limited, don't exaggerate that skill set.)

Communication Skills

I have excellent or proficient written and verbal communication skills in both English and Spanish. (If you are not bi-lingual, look into it!)

Education / Certifications

I hold a _____ or I'm currently pursuing my degree in _____, or I'm a high school graduate, and I am currently pursuing higher education (all are acceptable statements).

Characteristics

I'm able to work under pressure, I enjoy working with people, and I am detail oriented.

ZIP!!! Your!!! LIPS !!! and SMILE!!!

Weaknesses

Write out your weaknesses and turn them into strengths. Pay attention to the way these statements are written. They can become powerful tools.

Ex: I get irritated by disorganization in filing. — I'm a stickler for files being put back where they belong.

Ex) My kindness gets mistaken for a weakness. — I am a very kind person who works well with others.

Ex) I have been told I am not social enough at work. — I am very job-focused.

Strengths:

These are the positive qualities that you possess. Beef 'em up and sell yourself!

Ex: My ability to communicate in a multi-cultural environment translates into productive and friendly work relationships with others that add to the bottom line.

Again, know what skills are necessary for the industry you are applying in.

The question they may ask you:

"Where do you see yourself in five years?" (You are applying your skills within their company, so never say you want to own your own company.) A good answer is, "With the proper training and the right opportunity, I would like to be a part of the management team and work with people like you."

** Take the One Minute Commercial and record it on your cell or home phone voice mail. It will allow you easy access to the proven job obtaining format. **

One Minute Commercial Format

There are three things they want to know when they lay eyes on you. Les Brown teaches this fantastic concept that assists anyone in understanding how to build a powerful personal brand.

- ➢ Who are you?
- ➢ Why are you here?
- ➢ Why should I care?

You must have the ability to communicate this information effectively in a timely fashion. It will put you in the position of a well-polished presenter showing your skills and abilities.

Below are the top five questions to ask before you enter an interview.

On the phone:

- ➢ When I arrive, who will I report to?
- ➢ If downtown, do you validate parking?
- ➢ When do you expect to fill this position?
- ➢ What is your hiring process?
- ➢ Who will I be interviewing with? (This may sound redundant, but you will often be reporting to the receptionist and be seen by a hiring manager or HR staff.)

Questions to ask during an interview:

- ➤ If hired, who will I report to?
- ➤ What is the typical workday like?
- ➤ When do you expect to fill this position?
- ➤ What is your hiring process?
- ➤ What are the benefits of a full-time salaried position and are any bonuses given?
- ➤ Do you enjoy working for this company and what is the corporate culture like?

Day 11

Practice

One Minute Commercial

 ➤ Top five questions to ask script
 ➤ Record this on your cell phone voicemail.

Draft a closing interview script:

"Mrs. Jones, I would like to thank you for your time. I feel that with my skills and abilities, I'm a great fit for this position. I look forward to being a part of your team. When can I expect to hear from you?"

Practice this closing statement, and you will leave a lasting impression on the interviewer.

Day 12

** *Salary Negotiation Research* **

Things to research:

> ➤ The size of the company.
> ➤ Geographical location of the company's headquarters.
> ➤ Competitors within the industry.
> ➤ Financial projection and growth.
> ➤ Where they are branded within the industry.
> ➤ How much of the market share they dominate?

Go to salary.com and Google.com and search "sample salary profile." From this, you should have a good indication of the industry standard for your particular career field.

Become comfortable with what you think you are worth as it relates to the compensation package you desire. You know what is required to take care of your household. Remember, the amount you are requesting should reflect the value you bring to the company. Executive individuals calculate the rate of return on investment and have subconsciously made a decision in their minds about your worth, know that.

Day 13

Salary Negotiation Pitch

Any questions about salary should be asked when you are confident with your interview presentation. Now that they understand you will be a good return on investment, wait until the end to ask about compensation.

Question: What is the salary you have budgeted for this position?

The person that asks the question is the person who controls the conversation, but they may answer your question with a question. You may be asked, "What is the salary that you are requiring?"

The most dominant answer is:

"Through my research I understand the industry standard for the _____ position within the_____ industry is between_____ and_____ . With my_____ years of experience, skills and expertise

~ 75 ~

within the industry, I'm sure we can come to an agreement that we are both comfortable with."

Now go back and briefly recap the information you gave with confidence in your One Minute Commercial to close the deal.

If the person you are talking to is not the decision maker, then you stop there. If you are talking to the decision maker, giving a salary range between _-

_____ and _____it will keep you from exposing your collective bargaining agreement amount. Remember, this is a negotiation. You are there to get the maximum compensation package for your business partnership.

Day 14

Study the Salary Section

Practice questions and pitch with a partner or try practicing with an audio recording from your voice mail.

Day 15

Personal Meeting with a Career Coach or Trusted Advisor

Formal Mock Interview

Review your resumes, cover letter and reference sheet. Memorize your pitch statement

Personal Video of Session

At this meeting, your power suit should be worn and bring everything you need for the interview. Competition is fierce and you must be prepared.

Day 16

How to Network Effectively

Business card approach: order business cards from vistaprint.com. These cards are cost-effective and a great way to stay productive by handing out something professionally printed with your name, career information and several means by which you can be contacted. But that means you have to answer your phone and check your emails.

Research networking circles in your area.

Ex: Woman's/Men's Business Associations

> ➢ Industry-specific organizations
> ➢ Contacts from your networking list

Day 17

Master the Madness

At this point, every segment of your informational scripts should be memorized.

Master the art of the One Minute Commercial along with:

> ➤ The top five questions to ask on the phone.
> ➤ The top five questions to ask at the interview.
> ➤ Your salary negotiation pitch.
> ➤ Your closing the interview statement.

Day 18

Setting up the Interviews

Make appointments to interview with career placement agencies. They can set up interviews with industry-specific companies for you. These placement agencies interview you the same way any other company will. If you don't take them seriously, you will become just a piece of paper in the sea of nobodies. Align yourself with prominent agencies that hire in your career field. Now you need to put into action everything you have learned up to this point.

It's essential while job hunting to consider a part-time job. This will assist you with internal emotional leverage as you get ready to negotiate. Part-time employment will help drive revenue for your company while you are still in the research stages of getting appointments with the larger companies.

Commit:

Two hours daily of Internet searches through job search databases.

Locate projected job fairs you will attend and remember, don't just attend a job fair to participate.

Job fairs are designed to get a massive assessment of what is available for projected companies. They are being used to fulfill several purposes:

> - To help job seekers get a bird's-eye view of the competition in various industries.
> - To help companies get an idea of what the job-seeking public looks and sounds like.
> - To provide networking for many businesses and agencies.

There is an economic impact from the participants that need a job, including money from venue parking lots, gas stations and restaurants. They are all making money off this massive unemployment explosion.

Day 19

Morning Teleconference and do a Mock Interview

Day 20

Listen to the CD "Think and Grow Rich" by Napoleon Hill

Day 21

Study the Internet for additional job options in case your current plan falters.

Day 22

Meet with a Personal Consultant

Prepare for the job interview, engage in an intensive job search effort, and listen to a motivational audio series.

Day 23

Stress Management

- ➢ What types of stresses are there?
- ➢ How do you overcome stress in your life?
- ➢ How do you eliminate stress?
- ➢ What are some myths about unemployment stress?

Day 24

Q & A

Refer to your initial goal sheet for setting short-term employment goals. Also set long-term career goals.

- ➢ What is your ideal job opportunity?
- ➢ What type of career have you always dreamed about?
- ➢ What location do you want to work in?
- ➢ What type of atmosphere do you want to work in?
- ➢ What type of people do you want to work with?

Day 25

Check out Recommended Book Listings

You should read books or listen to books via your car or MP3 player that will stimulate your work ethic and move you to the next level.

Day 26

Revisit and Create

The Entrepreneur Mentality will create a follow-up system with different ways to close an interview.

Day 27

Making Career Decisions

Do an overview of your part-time employment options. These can be viewed as opportunities that can open doors and build new relationships with other productive, driven people. Again, it's about a secure network of "door openers."

Day 28

Your Dream Job

By now your confidence should be red hot. Your adrenaline should be pumping enough to light up an entire city block. Take this energy, go through your contact list, and let everyone know you are ready for your dream job!

Name six significant things you want to accomplish within the next thirty days and answer the following questions:

> ➢ What will it bring to you if you find a job?
> ➢ Who will be affected by you having a job?
> ➢ How badly do you want to find a job?
> ➢ How many people do you know that can help you find a job?

Day 29

Take the day relax and do something fun. It will relieve all the stress you have faced over the last twenty-eight days.

Day 30

The Job is Yours

The job is yours. You make a difference. You are the real asset.

"Live Your Dreams—Today is Your Day!"–*Lizzy McNett*

About the Author

Anna provides it all as if you are in the saddle along for the journey. Her rare books bring the readers joy from nearly every genre they can appreciate. She exuberantly brings the image and sentiments of the west to full life throughout the storyline. Yet, at the core of Judd's work is a black stallion who engages life into every aspect of the book. Haystack fills children's minds with wonder as he interacts with Marshal Spur and the Outrider Gang, to the mild minored young steed who brings Adam to new levels of learning in his life. Then he is brilliantly portrayed as a beautiful Appaloosa stallion in the Broncobuster as Cash.

Anna is one of the greatest novelists and a freelance ghostwriter is known for equestrian professionalism in every genre. Her young adult fiction novels and all books bring joy to the readers.

Lizzy is the founder of Writers Publishing House/Ghost Writer Media, who writes under her pen name Anna Elizabeth Judd, a solid publishing firm with more than a decade of assisting clients will their publishing needs. She has a BA in fine arts, with a minor in Equine Science. On the side, she studied at Scottsdale Art Institute under Robert 'Shoofly' Shufelt.

Lizzy writes books, which considering this website, makes perfect sense. She is best known for ghostwriting various best sellers in all genres. Along with her novels based on the initial part of her working career, horse training. As she understands the importance of family values, Lizzy chose a pen name borrowed from her family tree, Anna Elizabeth Judd.

When not absorbed in writing for clients, Lizzy can be found hiking, biking, or any outside activity. Although she does not train horses any longer, their spirits will always be a part of her soul. As a passionate entrepreneur Lizzy understands the importance of exemplary customer service, it is the basis for any successful business. In this case, Writers Publishing House was founded on the idea that the focus must be on the client's success. She believes, "Everyone should profit from their passion."

If you want to know more about publishing a book, please visit her website at https://writerspublishinghouse.com where you can contact her about starting your book project today.

Anna's Books: annaelizabethjudd.com

- The Power of Thought
- IAuthor – Social Media Marketing Guide
- The Broken Angel
- IAM – Guide to Self-Realization **coming soon….**
- The Handbook of Horsemanship
- The Broncobusters
- The Hourglass of el Diablo

- Marshal Spur and the Outlaw
- The Boy Who Couldn't Talk
- Spur Up! – Music Album
- Hey, Hay Learn Your ABC's
- Learn Your ABCs with Haystack

- A Distant Calling
- Skimmer's Adventure

www.ingramcontent.com/pod-product-compliance
Lightning Source LLC
Chambersburg PA
CBHW071502210326
41597CB00018B/2663